The Essentia

Selected and New Works

 Most of the poems in this volume have been previously published, either as part of a prior collection or in print or online journals including *The Boston Globe, Worcester Review, Muddy River Poetry Review, Constellations, Rye Whiskey Review, Boston Literary Magazine, sPoKe, Harvard Mosaic, Mass Poetry, North of Oxford, Meanie, Turtle Island Quarterly, Compassion Anthology, First Literary East, Blue Pepper Review* and others.

ISBN: 978-1-945917-62-2

Printed in the United States of America

Photo illustration and cover design by
Christopher Reilley in The Bytesized Studio

Also by Doug Holder:

Poems of Boston and Just Beyond: The Back Bay to the Back Ward
Dreams at the Au Bon Pain
Wrestling with my Father
The Man in the Booth in the Midtown Tunnel
Eating Grief at 3 A.M.
Portrait of an Artist as a Young Poseur: Boston 1974 – 1983
Last Night at the Wursthaus

"Making other books jealous since 2004"

Big Table Publishing Company
Boston, MA and San Francisco, CA
www.bigtablepublishing.com

REVIEWS

"The landscape has changed but the memories haven't. Take a walk with these poems that bring back the old Harvard Square, Boston, and the Bronx…step back into time with the characters Doug Holder describes all contemplating their dead ends and new beginnings."

~ Gloria Mindock, *The Whiteness of Bone*

"Threadbare and fedora-dashing, Doug Holder maneuvers through cityscapes of judgmental blondes, beheaded voyeurs, and dead men needing affection, Along the way, Holder studies the solemn detritus that people inevitably shed, like losing lottery tickets."

~ Dennis Daly, *Sentinel*

"No one delivers the sharp, sweet bite of nostalgia like Doug Holder. You'll find yourself transported back to the days when everything was fascinating and each person you met had a story— the ancient, surly waitress barking out orders, to the blondes who always had the power to intimidate."

~ Robin Stratton, *Some Have Gone and Some Remain*

"This book is a jewel; multifaceted, scintillating, and completely unique. There is not a wasted word within the covers."

~ Christopher Reilley, *One Night Stanza*

"With reflective humor, he unfolds moments of insight amid vernal uncertainty. The vignettes are enticing, fondly resonating time and place."

~ Richard Fox, *embracing the burlesque of collateral damage*

"The writing is pointed, unpretentious and honest, providing snapshots of rough-edged jobs and unvarnished people, places in Boston that have vanished, historical snippets on the street, in restaurants and subways."

~ Nina R. Alonso, *Constellations Magazine*

"A unique memoir, in poetry, of a real Boston artist looking back at a distinct point in time at a city I love. The man, the city, the book are all completely unique, wonderful and original."

~ Timothy Gager, *Spreading Like Wildflowers*

"Doug Holder's poems incise surgically, expertly, to the failing heart of human experience and gets it beating again, and then sets it dancing."

~ Alan Kaufman, *The Drunken Angel*

"One of those rare collections with every poem as delicious as the stack of syrup-saturated pancakes you used to tuck into at Bickford's in the wee hours of the morning. (You were just a kid—in your twenties—and didn't get indigestion, and the coffee didn't keep you awake all night or make you get up ten times to pee.) On the menu are poems that nail the groove of those days. The writing, of course, is breathtaking; stylish and elegant, like the cook himself, but with the unexpected bite of an otherwise polite terrier. But poets beware! You will be jealous! Possibly suicidal! Remember how Beach Boy Brian Wilson was partway through what he envisioned would be the greatest rock album of all time when he heard *Sgt. Pepper*? He ditched *Smile* and went into seclusion for about a decade. Reading Doug Holder is kind of like that."

~ *Boston Literary Magazine*

"Doug Holder is above all an urban poet, an observer chronicling the everyday sights and absurdities of Somerville, Boston and New York City in plain talk flavored with cool irony and sudden startling bursts of imagery. His settings include hospital rooms, bars, coffee shops, Harvard Yard, the post office, buses and subway trains, the Boston Public Library, Shea Stadium, housing projects, city streets, and the Midtown Tunnel from Queens to Manhattan. His characters are bizarre and ordinary like all of us. I'm reminded in the pages of this collection of meeting, a year or two before her death, the artist Alice Neel, who painted gorgeously surreal ironic portraits of famous and ordinary people in the 1930s and 40s—and shivering as she looked me over. Doug Holder looks at the world through a similarly sharp and amused set of eyes. Yet there is no malice but a profound sympathy here—for the helplessness of aging and of poverty, for physical and mental illnesses, for the complexity of family relations—and most of all, for the isolation and loneliness lurking underneath tenaciously crowded city life. However, let me assure you this is not a gloomy collection of poems. There are rich nuggets of humor and wry reflection throughout this collection and, to combat the isolation of urban life, in almost every poem a relationship is forged between the observing eye and the subject of the poem."

~ Pamela Annas, *A Disturbance in Mirrors: The Poetry of Sylvia Plath.*

"Holder finds something almost like beauty or knowledge in the abandoned warehouses with weeds crawling to the roof. There are always dreams, even if never fulfilled. There is so often the sense of time passing, of letting go— letting go of people, letting go of Harvard Square Theater and the Wursthaus, balms that seemed like they would always be there. And they are and always will be in Holder's moving poems."

~ Lyn Lifshin, *Cold Comfort*

"Doug Holder writes poetry with a passion and insight that deserves prestige and influence all its own."

~ S. Craig Renfroe, Jr., *Main Street Rag Magazine*

"A master poet who sees the world clearly and shares that vision generously with readers."

~ Laurel Johnson, *Midwest Book Review*

"A great poet and a Boston legend."

~ Joe Gouveir, host of *Poet's Corner*, Provincetown Radio

"From toilets to pay phones, to the fluid connection to all things human is utterly Doug Holder and there isn't anyone out there remotely doing what (he does) so beautifully…so dryly and always with human regard."

~ Linda Larson, former editor-in-chief of *Spare Change News*

"Kudos for this grand effort that makes us wish that we were the author of these poems."

~ Harris Gardner, *Lest They Become*

"Go get this book. Take it home. Savor it."

~CD Collins, *Self Portrait with Severed Head*

ACKNOWLEDGEMENTS

My wife Dianne Robitalle, my mother Rita Holder, my talented and generous brother Donald Holder, my sister-in-law Evan Yionoulis, Jennifer Matthews, Harris Gardner, Lainie Senechal, Steve Glines, Robert K. Johnson, Lawrence Kessenich, Zvi Sesling, Karen Klein, Timothy Gager, Christopher Reilley, the late Donald Norton, Bobie Toner, Dr. Dan Sklar, Dr. Mark Herlihy, Dennis Daly, Rose Gardenia, Deborah Priestly, Emily Pineau, Gloria Mindock, Kirk and Lucy (my talented next door neighbors), Linda Conte, Renuka Raghavan, all the Bagel Bards, the staff, past and present of the Ibbetson Street Press, Endicott College and so many others.

Special thanks go to Robin Stratton, who very fortunately badgered me into doing the book and did a wonderful job of putting it all together.

INTRODUCTION

While writing this introduction to Doug Holder's "essential" collection, I was tempted to toss out all my verbiage and just quote line after line after line from his poems. They're that good. And they get to what is essential to him and to all of us—mortality.

But his poems aren't gloomy or preachy like the ubiquitous Latin medieval poems known as *memento mori*: remembering death. Holder's poems are vitally full of life, irony, astute observations, side-long glances of humor. Even when there is an ending, there is, most always, a qualification making the ending less absolute, as in the poem which commemorates an iconic restaurant, "Jacob Wirth (Boston, Mass. 1868 to 2019)": *What once was alive in this city/is still/not quite/dead.* "Unknown in a Crowd": *Observing/not observed,* the poet thinks, in that circumstance, *he can "almost—/tolerate/them all.* With words like "quite" and "almost," the poet avoids stark alternatives: alive/dead or reject/tolerate and finds his way to evade absolutes.

Whether he tolerates them all or not, Holder's observational skills are magnificent and magnanimous in his generous, wide-ranging embrace of our common humanity. Although his short lines and complex line breaks are nowhere like Whitman's, his inclusive scope of persons and places is, and ranges from "Teenagers at The Mall *doing the twist/with their fingers/on their cell phones*; to *a man at Ratner's whose life has been/reduced to yelling at a round shouldered/waiter, "you call this a pickle!"* to his dying friend in "Lung Cancer: Stage 4" whose only wish, if he could do his life over, was that *my parents/had sent me to a private school.* The incongruity of the dying man's wish, considering the situation, shows the poet's skillful use of juxtaposition to temper sorrow with humor, as well as his ability to listen well and capture the perfect detail.

Holder's mastery of the art of the detail is convincingly evident in the cascading plethora of descriptions from *Portrait of An Artist as a Young Poseur 1974-1983.* Grounding details of his personal life in the exact places they happened, he gives us a map of Boston's Ends and Squares, Streets and Avenues, where his various jobs were, where his preferred foods—hot dogs at Buzzy's croissants at Savoy Bakery, roast duck at Ying-Ying, the dark beers and dark bars and the women in them, and in the mental hospital where he worked the night shift; all the characters with their voices: *what's it going to be, hon, I can't stand all this eating! Look at this fuckin' character.*

There is theatricality in these energy-driven, tumble of associations organized only by place as their titles indicate. In "Ken's Deli in Copley Square" there's the fat manager, the rotisserie chicken, the dishwasher, drag queens in the men's room, the waitress, and actors off from a gig. Shakespeare's claim "all the world's a stage" could describe these scenes, and all in them become characters. If Shakespeare's right, we're all players and can imagine ourselves into some of those scenes—the *loneliness/made visible* in the bars at 3 A.M., the fire alarm driving us from our apartments—the beautiful chaos of these dramas, the astonishing voices of ordinary life bring us intimately into the poems.

Even the poet sees himself as a *late night character* or in a Thornton Wilder play. Naming himself a "Poseur," like an actor, he has clothing props: a Filene's Basement jacket, red scarf, beret which cannot enhance his narrow shoulders, flabby body, skinny neck, thinning hair. He mocks the absurdity of his attempt to bolster his frail ego. But he does not mock his desire to be a writer, to be with poets and writers, to have his own Algonquin. Discovering the Beat poets and their promise of freedom from conformity, he continues his journal entries, *trying to construct a narrative of the chaos of my life.*

Holder's sense of self is complex and fluid. Unsparing in his self-descriptions, he could be the monster as the child on the bus sees him, or *I saw myself on the Dudley bus that day* when the poet sees a stranger *that man/perhaps me.* A reflection? Another life he imagines he might have? An identification with a stage character, "I Am Willy Loman" from Arthur Miller's *Death of a Salesman*—the play's title never specifically mentioned but immediately associated—could be a mixture of himself and his father. Doug Holder, both the person and the poet, is a daily walker all over the city. Like a salesman making his rounds *to shoot the same old shit/another round of pitches* the poet says, half humorously, half seriously, *They love me, they love me in Somerville*, Holder's hometown. And they do.

The most incongruous, semi-serious merging of identities is the poet walking on Truro Beach, followed by an old crab: *we were both in our shells/ suspicious narrow slits of eyes.* Whether we can read the crab "shell" image as indicative of the poet's sense of himself or just his astrological sign, there is a restraint in these poems, an avoidance of emotional verbal extravagance while depicting disturbing material. Holder's detailed descriptions of the deaths of two men, one on the locked ward, the other on the Red Line, conclude with ironic comments which leave us smiling, not sorrowful. His poetic skill in presenting Diane Arbus' photo of the eleven year old girl *trapped in a crocheted/ cocktail dress/ a child/forced in a cage/ of carnal contours*—repetitive alliteration emphasizes her entrapment, the densely-suggestive adjective "carnal" indicates both her body and the viewers' perversity—distances us a bit from the photo's awfulness as we admire the poet's craft. Distancing has no part in his concise evaluation of his father's apologetic words while getting his morning vodka *Captured in dementia/ and the maudlin*, maudlin a place Holder never goes. His tone is consistently multiple: wary, clear-eyed, unsparing, rarely judgmental, ironically generous, sharply witty with undertones of sadness. If there is bitterness, it is tempered by compassion.

Both compassion and restraint combine in the poems about his nonagenarian mother. Most women can identify with her cry of "Where is My Pocketbook?": her fear of losing it, her *flimsy thread/ to hold onto*, as encroaching dementia prevents her from knowing she holds it. The poet refrains from describing his emotional reaction to his mother's cries not to suffer or her wish to die. This poem is about her, not him, about her pocketbook; but his detailed description of its contents shows what careful attention he is paying to her. Some adjectives verge toward humor: *errant lipstick*, *deceased phone numbers*; language, adroitly used, deflects tears.

But there are his tears, *barely* contained, in the poem about his father's *shrunken frame*, his difficult urination. The pathos of old age, the failed dreams, the inability to *face the dark* when death is not an abstraction—no ironic relief or humor here. "Wrestling with My Father", the title of one section of poems, indicates the complexities of that relationship, the unending problematics of understanding it through poetry. "At Benson's Deli with Dad" reaches deep and comes up with treasure. Beginning with their failed attempt *two Jews* awkwardly tossing a football to fulfill some All-American father/son ritual *that neither had any belief in*, the poem moves to a luscious description of the deli food consumed by the poet, his father and brother, the pleasure they feel generously shared with the readers. The scene concludes, as many of Holder's poems do, with an insight: *And for me/ those afternoons/ that warm nostalgic hue/ is all/ that rings true.*

That may be all that rings true for Doug Holder, but so much of what he has written rings true for his readers; resonates with them. One of my favorites, and a surprise, is "Canned," a serious subject presented with imagination and wit—pure Doug Holder. Who else could write a poem about tinned fish? The haunting fear of the dead rat's carcass, death's symbol, doesn't shadow this poem; the fish are already dead. They have experienced *terminal canning*, an unusually humorous way of thinking about the role of coffins. Death is obviated, no longer fearful because it's already happened. The poet moves on to attempt a description of their *predicament* in the tin, and decides no poetic flourishes, just the facts: *packed in, like, well,/ what they are.* In a brilliant move, Holder anthro-pomorphizes these fish (I'm assuming sardines) and wonders *what school/ of thought they/ were in*, punning on the usual term for the swimming formation of small fish and the term used for Greek philosophers and Peripatetics in their different schools of thought. The poem moves away from death to speculate about what was happening before their canning, *what were they planning?* A very important question for us to ponder—what are we planning?—and one which he could, and probably does, ask of many of the characters that swim in his poems.

Drinking coffee in "My Mother Prepares Me for Death", she and her son sit *In silence/ we have said it all—*; the poet adds in a kind of throwaway dismissal *more or/ less.* But there is more. These poems are for grownups, whatever their chronological age.

Read them and find out. You'll be very glad you did.

~ Karen Klein, Retired Brandeis Professor,
Founder of **teXtmoVes**, a poetry/dance collaborative.

TABLE OF CONTENTS

POEMS OF BOSTON AND JUST BEYOND: THE BACK BAY TO THE BACK WARD

DREAMS AT THE AU BON PAIN

WRESTLING WITH MY FATHER

THE MAN IN THE BOOTH IN THE MIDTOWN TUNNEL

EATING GRIEF AT 3 A.M.

PORTRAIT OF AN ARTIST AS A YOUNG POSEUR BOSTON 1974 – 1983

LAST NIGHT AT THE WURSTHAUS

NEW

The Essential Doug Holder
Selected and New Works

POEMS OF BOSTON AND JUST BEYOND: THE BACK BAY TO THE BACK WARD

Daddy, Is He a Monster?

A child caught sight of me on a bus
propped up on his seat
safe within his father's fold
he said
"Is he a monster?"

My head
poking out of a protective shell of newspaper
a suspicious crab
peering at a threatening predator
my blood shot eyes squinting
behind a shield of dark glass.
the top of my head
devoid of hair
shining under an aura of artificial light
from the vehicle.
an unruly beard
sprouted
tinted with gray
from my flushed cheeks.

I forced a smile
the child screamed
and disappeared behind his seat

Byron

What will he wear this morning?
A Greek fisherman's hat
or the white captain's cap
will he hobble with the clear plastic cane
carrying the African statuettes—
porcelain cats with hollow eyes
holding his hand out
an excited child at show and tell
to show you their size

Will he be the grumpy old man…
railing against the world
this cold morning
cursing the homeless…lecherously eyeing the young girls
mourning how his wife let herself go
the too ample rump
the sagging bust
the gray hair
how she mirrors him
he blinds himself.

Will he be my friend this morning?
The private jokes
jocular slaps on the back
his tongue in his cheek.

Will he be the doting father
the unsolicited advice
world weary wisdom
sad truths
continued hope.

What will he be this morning?
What shall I?

Fallen Cherub Outside the Liquor Store

A rainy night
with the sudden wasted light of the store's neon sign.
I saw him
first his head
his crown topped with a manicured puff of cream-colored curls
swirling into each other
like the top of some celebratory cake
supported by the abrupt ends of his crew cut
rising from the sides of his head

He turned his face towards me—
a smiling mouth
that had turned cruel
still with the fleshy, flushed cheeks of a choir boy.

He inhaled on his cigarette
captured in a fresco
of smoky, wet mist
floating in a menthol cloud.

A Moose in Boston

I saw it trot
down Commonwealth Avenue
its majestic head
dour and pinched
with patrician bearing
covering the same ground
that horses of lesser lineage
plodded over years before.

It strode
alongside the subway car
with the precision of dancers' legs
looking discreetly at the window frames
of peoples' faces
like a museum of surprise.

I heard it snort
in the humid air
its head upturned
fighting an assault to its dignity
gracefully disappearing in the bush
as if to shake a patch of persistent flies
the police
hot on its tail.

A Wind Down Boylston Street

It blew the café's umbrella
aloft
the rarefied advertisement
on the brim
splayed on the concrete
destroying any pretensions
their droll flap in the languid breeze
just moments ago.
Pedestrians—
cool silk shirts
ballooned
like bombastic clowns
distorting the hard-earned symmetry
of their polished bodies.
The wind pushed the along
intolerant of fashionable posturing
breaking
their elegant gaits
to halting shuffles.

Now…
they stood braced
for another bout
but…
it would not give them the satisfaction.

Cigarette on the Psychiatric Ward

"Can I have a light?"

What was the sudden spark in her eyes,
that flame
from cloudy, dormant pupils,
when I lit her cigarette?

The sudden, driving ambition
to inhale,
the sunken chest's almost boastful expansion.
The smoke filling the yawning cavity.
A woman of substance …
until she exhaled.

At the Reading: Young Poet

She illuminated the dark bar
like the distant
pristine light from the maw of a cave.
Her expression
practiced, dramatic
but every so often
betraying herself
with a nervous tic
a flutter of her eyes
an awkward positioning of her legs.

She talked of making love
as if a new discovery
of how he fills her crevices
she is he
or he is she
couplings in small rooms
of old Cambridge victorians
cigarette smoke
lipstick traces
romantics places
half-empty glasses
the lingering scent
remembered words…
phrases.

Looking at the audience
her body willowy
graceful
her face impervious to the revealing glare of the spotlight
her hair dropping down her shoulders
looking like was glazed with honey.

From the corner
an old woman
lifted her head
from the rim of her shot glass
and cackled
breaking the spell:
"What's the big deal, kid, and two dogs could do that."

The Welterweight

On the locked ward
in his corner
hunched into a permanent boxer's stance
his head twisted into a violent right angle
his features pained
from an ancient echo of a punch—
the elderly pugilist
springs into action with the ring of the fire alarm bell
sparring with us
ducking and weaving
around our dead-end grabs.
"I'll go a full eight,"
he mutters to himself.

The bell ceases
we lead him back to his neutral corner
and drape a towel
over his skeletal shoulders
wiping the spittle
from the sides of his mouth.

He smiles at us
raising his arms slowly in triumph
his blue veins
mapped under a thin sheath of skin.

We wheel him down the corridor
his boxer shorts losing their grip
dropping below his diminished waist
his torso dwarfed under a shower towel,
"Better luck next time, boys!"

First Night on the Job on the Psychiatric Ward

The night seemed perfectly cast…
stormy, thunder and rain
the patient was biblical
long hair and a beard
with his staff at his command.

He put a paternal hand on me
and called me his finest creation
what could I do but thank him?
He smiled
with divine patronization
undoubtedly I was a much-valued acolyte.

Then suddenly
a flash from the storm lit the building
in a momentary spectral glow
a clap of thunder howled down the locked ward.

He looked at me like a proud teacher
patting me on the back.
"Good work, kid. Good work."

DREAMS AT THE AU BON PAIN

Unknown in a Crowd

And that's when
you felt most at peace—
lost in the cornucopia.
Feeling
like the multi-eyed
fly on the wall
away from the claustrophobic intimacy.
Observing
not observed
owner of your own dialogue…

You think—
for once—
you can—
almost—
tolerate
them all.

Au Bon Pain at Dusk

You know the skids
when the *Spare Change* hawker
won't call you "young man"—
when the haunts
you slipped into
like an old shoe
are boarded
with angry wood crosses
when the glance of a beatific
Harvard girl
escapes you
with a bothered flick of her head.

You sit at a table
in the courtyard of the café
brittle autumnal leaves
rest,
then tumble off your round shoulders…
they just don't hold
what they used to.

It is dusk…
your knees ache clandestinely
under the table.
The prospect of sleep
awaits you
like the promise
of a young night
once did.

The Last Smoke

And I knew better…
to flirt,
to watch
the trail
of seductive
smoke
coil
around me.
To feel—
the pleasure
the warm
fatal rush
ashes on
my breath.

What were
my gestures
without it?
hanging languidly
from my fingers
contemplating
the ceiling—
punctuating
the before
the after,
the hello …
good-bye.

Photo

The picture—
faded—
a yellowish tint—
"Nov. 1965"
an afterthought
on its backside.
My brother—
holding an autumnal leaf
almost a template
to his small hand.
The leaf
was brittle
with twisted veins
the rich green
the ripe bursts of color
dimmed
to a somber brown.
I remember that leaf
slipping
from his grip
with a gust
of wind
he would retrieve it…
Much later.

A Lucien Freud Nude

Her head thrown back
in abandon—
the legs like
generous thick shanks
of beef.
The breasts—
large and flat
lay deflated
on the
corpulent folds
of her stomach.
What does she welcome?
Or welcomed?
Spread
like pastry lard
on a couch
looking to the heavens
for some
piercing answer
through the
barriers
of undulating
flesh.

The Love Life of J. Edgar Hoover

The breeze crumples
your sheer caftan…
mother downstairs
off her rocker
your loyal assistant
straddles you
and in your ecstasy
your bulldog face
creased with effeminate screams
reveling
with your little agent's
successful probe
the stiff penetration through the muck
deeper and deeper
into your stagnant well…
reamed
clean
you sleep
with his
gentle kiss.

3 A.M. on the Psychiatric Ward

My flashlight beamed
on the usual bed-bound bodies
breathing under layers.
then—
in the middle of the hall
she came running toward me
perfect, unblemished…naked
a nocturnal melodrama unfolding
the embodiment of a wet dream.
Her eyes beamed
sensitive as a doe's—
then she lunged for me—
I grabbed both of her arms
and we did our strange dance
anointed by moonlight
from the barred window
tripping the light fantastic—
I was frightened and thrilled,
as she took the lead.

Leaving the Way He Came In

He died
curled in a fetal position
eyes frozen in wonderment
a question mark
achieving its long-sought closure.

I saw the signs
along the way
his body turning in on itself
his hands clenched at his side
cramped into blunt fists
the square shoulders
arcing downward
forming a hump of heavy burden.

The years
left him
a wizened infant
with wisps of fine gray hair
springing from his scalp
as if
to finally transcend him.

I sat beside his hospital bed
a prison of metal rails
a terminal crib
where he was nursed in shifts
breast fed with IV tubes
lulled to sleep
by the beep of the incessant monitor.

He passed
mouth gaping
wearing the indignity of a diaper
navel gazing
into eternity.

The Death of Bernie M.

I remember
it was his typical saunter
down the locked ward
the vague
cusp of a smile
a black,
shopworn suit
looking like a down-at-the-heels
clergyman,
the benign muttering
for yet another
cigarette.

And so suddenly
his mouth gaping
at the ceiling
his eyes
already devoid of life
the machine
throwing shocks
through his vacant
body—
How delighted he
would be
to see a pretty nurse
covering his mouth
with her full lips
the surprise with me—
straddling him
pressing desperately
on his chest…

What a shame
all this…
waited
for his
corpse.

On the Ward: Stuffed Animals

At night
as you
check the rooms
the flashlight discovers
these animals
attached to grown
women—
like suckling babes
held tightly
against the darkness—
memories of morning
abandonment—
the deep chasms
that were never
bridged.
On these lonely
nights
any union
will do

WRESTLING WITH MY FATHER

Whitestone Bridge, NY, 1963

Sunday afternoons.
The bridge
to the Bronx
a spurt of connective tissue.
Bridging a new limb
to an old.
The rusted welcome sign:
"Bronx, Beach and Pool."
A decaying smile glistening
in the summer sun.

I looked at my parents
in the rearview—
their gimlet eyes
blue slits—
Crow's feet
creased in intimate smiles,
meeting the tenement's eruption
on the other side.

They were homing pigeons
with compelling instinct
for continual return.

My brother and I
wrapped in silence
in the back.
Dancing with the taunting
sense of the seminal
beyond our limited reach

At Benson's Deli with Dad

Father and I
awkwardly threw a football
back and forth—
our forced theatrics
two Jews
in some tortured
Rockwellian pantomime
that neither had any belief in.

It was in Benson's Deli
on Saturday afternoons
with the pop and long-awaited fizz
of the Doctor Brown's,
the delicious hint of
vanilla cream
at the cusp of my nostril.

Dad's loving adornment
of his hotdog
a true work of abstract art—
a colorful phallus
of juice and savory meat.

And my brother and I
broke through the
brittle yellow casing
of a meat knish
as if we were
prospecting gold diggers.

And for me
those afternoons
that warm nostalgic hue
is all
that rings true

Wallace Ave., Bronx, 1965

Rows
of ancient Jewish mothers
like angry crustaceans
perched on lawn chairs
claws out
pinch at the peach fuzz
of my flushed cheeks.
I kiss the skin
above their leathery turkey necks
and listen to their
code of Yiddish.

Their generous breasts
withered by their offspring,
who
weaned on shtetl milk
now long beyond the pale
leave their mothers
to dry in the summer sun.

Now My Father Can't Eat Bagels

He no longer packs the bite.
His body can't stomach it.
Some things
won't pass
through the ulcerated passageway.
The sesame and poppy seeds
seek new fertile ground.
The lox has made its final run.
His sweet morning ritual,
his teeth pulling at the hot dough
his dry lips
lubricated
with a flood of butter.
The crust cresting
at the roof of his mouth
its unhindered descent.

Father's 3 A.M. Vigil

My room was more of a tomb
preserved mementos
settling in.
A sediment of summer camp pictures
orphaned snapshots
scattered around the room.

As I unpacked my bag
I could hear
the ancient, tribal
call of my father
from the backyard,
and my comic, Chaplinesque
descent down the staircase.
A chubby boy in pursuit
of a carbon-crusted meat
the sting of vinegar
on the roof of my mouth
from the fascist whip
of German potato salad

It is 3 A.M.
during my 38th year.
my elderly father's light
still burns
in his room.
He rubs the gray stubble
of his weathered cheeks,
so tired—
but still scheming
in the early hours,

still planning
another
assault on
Madison Ave—
afraid to turn the light out
and face the dark.

He walks like the lonely
sentry he once was
during the "War"
between bedroom and bathroom.

I no longer hear
a youthful stream
pierce the water
all is tentative
and a struggle,
and I barely
can contain my tears
when I see
his shrunken frame

hunched over
pressing out
what is left of
him
so late
in the
night.

A Thought on Fathers' Day

And yes
it has come to the time
when I see my father's face
in the mirror.
My squint is his
the nascent crow's feet
stretching into laugh lines.
My angry brow
solicits the always surprising question
"What's wrong?"
"Why—nothing."
Didn't I always ask him
the same question?
Do I find myself
praying over the *New York Times*
like a scholar
over a sacred text?
A drink to my side
my legs crossed left to right
just like him?
Was that him the other day—
that reflection in
the store window—
slightly hunched
arms stiff
swinging robotically
clothed in Seersucker?
I looked back
but he was gone.

When Father Dies

When Father dies
let it
be in the midst
of the frenetic rush
of Madison Ave.
Let him fall like
a weathered pit bull
in a three-piece suit.

When father dies
stage his swan song
in a dark bar
with a dry martini
and an old pal.

When father dies
let it be on the rush hour
train home
his face buried
in the *Post*
his last breath involved
with the world.

When father dies
let it be
in front of the fireplace
with his wife,
talking to her
like she's still
the virginal student teacher
from the Bronx.

How are Things in the Sewer?

~ for Art Carney

My father shook with laughter
as that long, ungainly arm
reached into an archaic icebox
emerging with a flailing drumstick.

All his schemes
those madcap stabs
at so many
American dreams.

Those comic
Brooklyn catcalls
from an exotic, unseen
fire escape.

The weekly strange antic
dance with his corpulent pal
and I wonder
late at night
who can I really
laugh with now?

My Father's Fedora

Surprising
after dusting it off
it was the template
for my head.
The rakish angle
of the brim
was his—in an old snapshot.
And it seemed
the right time
to crown myself
with this weathered Stetson
and its understated
red feather.

And for a time
I swear
I felt
the brush
of his
warm
and ancient
hand.

THE MAN IN THE BOOTH IN THE MIDTOWN TUNNEL

Book Seducer

You have revealed
your subtext to me
in a hushed
intimate encounter.

I seduced you
on a train
lovingly
folding your
pages
with dog ears,
highlighting what
I loved about you
with deep
heart-red ink.

And even now
I talk you up
with people
I meet,
yet I abandoned you
on some commuter
rail seat.

The Family Picture

It has the smell of
decomposition.
Dog-eared
curled
sepia-tinted
fringes.
A moth-eaten family
rigidly positioned—
a hierarchy of rows.

Perhaps a maiden aunt,
her face
a dour, down-turned affair
relegated to the back.

and the two boys—
one looks defiantly at the camera
while the other
ponders the ground,

their vision
already in a cast
framed with barren winter branches
nothing will last.

Training Her Pet

She kept a tight
leash on him.
Pulling harder
when he strayed.

They walked through
the park
with the same clipped
brisk gait,
their eyes squarely
on the well-worn path.

Coming home
to the tasteful,
well-appointed living room—

And he knew his place,
scurrying to his usual corner.

She knew then
that they would be
ready to marry
soon.

Killing Time at the 99

~ a bar, like many bars, in Cambridge, MA

A skeletal man,
his torso
barely supports
a crispy white shirt
his forehead
violated by a jet black
wedge of his toupee

and a businessman's
perfunctory
flirtation
with the scripted chatter
of the barmaid.

(She assures us a few times
it is not the heat
but the humidity
that bothers her—)

He looks
to his
audience
staring into
the icy abyss
of his frosted glass.

An old man
pipes up
and fawns over
a prized cat
who I think
with such
suffocating attention
must be miserable,
and I drink
to all
this loneliness
made visible.

Private Dining Under a Blouse

~ for my nephew, Josh

In the middle of our conversation
and the din
of the large dining room
she lifted her blouse,
her baby blindly
grabbing her nipple
with his mouth.
The blouse covered him
like a shroud
for private dining.

I saw
the infant emerge
sleeping.
Held in an untroubled
dream.

I sucked on my straw,
flattening the plastic stem,
still awake
and troubled.

I Saw Myself on the Dudley Bus That Day

I saw myself on the Dudley bus that day,
his eyes: a blinking flirt
with the mid-winter's sun—
watching the slow fade
of a dying afternoon,
his face shadowed
in five o'clock.

Half-light,
no hair.
A bus of exiles
each mired
In their personal
Affairs.

And that man,
perhaps me?
looked a million
miles away.

I believe I saw
Him briefly yesterday
And for the first time
On that day
We saw each other
And quickly
Turned away.

Richard III in Hollywood

Richard
you are not over the hump—
the Armani suit
fits as tightly as a glove
highlighting your deformity—
a tumor
that stretches the expensive fiber.

Varicose veins cover you
like a road map
save the whites of
your dimmed eyes.

On your walk
along the strip
of your diminished kingdom
the lads on the corner
whisper
"Who's the gimp?"

The lady in the bar
rejecting your insidious advances
with an air of cultivation:
"Get lost, you ill-formed toad."

The ghosts that haunt you
vanished
now that you
popped the Prozac.

Yet…
in confidence
you tell me—
your singular audience
that you have deals to cut
evil to consummate
during your
Highly-rated
winter of discontent.

And I answer, intrigued:
"Hey—
Let's do lunch."

For Sarah

~ for my niece, Sarah Holder

And she ran.
Legs—
almost lifting her
into flight.
Eyes—
radiant
with wonder
not an inkling
of her
abrupt slide—

Her joyous romp
suddenly terminated—
flat
on her backside
and even in her father's
arms she cried.

She could never run that way again—
no matter how hard she tried.

Cambridge, MA: Two Old Women

Two old women
walk down
my street
each morning.

Lugging two
shopping bags
and two widow's humps.

Arm in arm
a tight embrace
of frail appendages
pushing each other
at no more
than a snail's pace.

Each morning
refusing the pull
of age's inertia.

A daily ritual
of decrepit defiance
walking the ground
that will own them.

The Life of the Party

Even the sparkling wine
seemed to wink
seductively at you.

After all,
you were
the center
the words
fell like pearls
from your mouth.

the approving smiles
from the women
the perfect opiate
delightful
but never enough.

And for this moment
you were a man
among the men
above—
out of reach
from the subtext
of their threats.
you weaved
through the crowd
like some predatory cat.

And then
in the bathroom mirror
who was this impostor
short and bald
struggling with
his fly

his eyes red-rimmed
and bulging
staring at you
in a comic assault
with your pants down.

You now
remembered your place.

Dianne at Sleep

~ for my wife, Dianne

As she lays
framed pictures
splashes of muted
color arise
from her
tousled head.

In her seep
she mutters
some B-
movie script
from her
nightly play,
while the
cat consumes her
with his
green eyes
a hungry
verdant blaze.

We both lay
just below
her breasts
and sleep
in a lap
for transient
treasured
guests.

His Last Impact on the Metropolis

~ *based on the* Boston Globe *account of a man who passed away on the* Red Line

When he passed
it was on the subway
the *Daily* dropped
from his hands.
His head
gave up its life-long
struggle with gravity.
He dropped
like some flimsy theatrical prop.
A middle-aged man,
his swan song
the indignity of
a comic roll on the floor—
the subway's screeching halt,
the trains backed up
From Cambridge to Dorchester.
Bulky, twisting
metal snakes.

The processional
with passengers
on either
side of the stretcher
watching some forgotten
ineffectual man
make his mark
freezing the rush hour
stopping them
dead in their
tracks.

A Dream of Minnie Baum

~ for my late grandmother, Minnie

I sit in the deep creases of her sundress,
a purple flourish of fabric flowers,
stunned by the musty cabal of her perfume.
My head resting on her soft deflated breasts.
She exchanges Yiddish for English with mother
tit for tat.

I am trapped…
My stomach leaden with chicken fat.
Bronx cheers from the pavement below.
I'm in familial ground
nesting in the lap
of a long-dead grandmother
with my mother's
jealous eyes
fixed on me.

Watching Her Read My Poem

Did I detect a smile
at the corner of her mouth?
She did hover on my page
A bit more than the others…

Obviously intelligent—
a creased noble brow
in the midst of an exegesis.
Folding the paper
for an exclusive focus on mine—
then standing
her proud purposeful gait
to the bus's door
then on to the street
and with perfect aim
right into
the trash.

The Last Hotdog

~ for Sy Baum

Long after he was hungry —
It was the last thing
He asked for
With any appetite.

She brought it
To his sick bed,
he bit through
The red casing
The familiar orgasm
Of juice
Hitting the roof
Of his mouth
In some facsimile
Of his youth.

Bites of memory:
The summer ballparks
The steam rising
From the carts
In warm, fragrant clouds
Against the shock
Of early spring cold

The mysterious, darkened
delicatessens
under the elevated tracks.
The Bronx gray afternoons
dining with his father.
The sullen
colorless meals
though the franks
fully garnished
the bright
yellow and green
of mustard
and relish.
He swallowed hard
it was all
too much
to digest.

Rat's Carcass

A deep blue sky
a sun bright
with its twelve o'clock high
summer with its largess
why must it be spoiled
by that dead rat's carcass?

Why,
when the long legs of ladies
pass in a tanned revue
does that rat's carcass
cruelly
come into view?

With my flesh so supple
my robust health not subtle
why must I see the rat's carcass?
What seems to be the trouble?

Heroin

To think
how his body
shed its ulcerated skin,
rested near the maw of death
sunning at the brink of the abyss.
Then to die
in the midst
of bliss.

EATING GRIEF AT 3 A.M.

Carpal Tunnel Syndrome

~ for my late father, Lawrence J. Holder

I thought of my father
as he gripped
his left hand
prying it open with his right
a hand curling
into a callused fetus
holding on to
something
for dear life.

And years after his death
as if possessed
I feel my own hand curling
in my right hand pocket
fusing with some phantom
in the darkness.

Eating Grief at Bickford's

~ for Allen Ginsberg

There are no places anymore
where I can sit at my threadbare table
pick at the crumbs on my plate
and wipe
the white dust
from my pitch
black shirt.

The old men
who used to spout
Marxist
rants from
the cracked porcelain of their cups
are gone.
The boiling water
ketchup soup
the mustard sandwich
they used to relish
all that so lean
cuisine.

Oh, Hunchback
in the corner
your lonely reflection
in the glass of water—

And Tennessee Williams' Blanche
eyes me through her grilled cheese
"Pass the sugar, sugar,"
she teases.

Maynard
the queer
late night
security guard.
His policeman's hat
draped on his head
looking like a
sacrilegious rake
his countless
renditions
of defending his honor
in the amorous, crazed embraces
of muscular young men
how he protests…
too much…too much.

The discarded men
blue blazers
shedding their threads
outcasts with newspapers.

Stains of baked beans
on their lapels
finger a piece
of passionless cod

lulled by their
own murmur.

Transcendence

I'm 84 floors up
but the city
doesn't seem to
make any more sense,
from my
exalted omnipotence.

A master lock
has chained my fluttering
heart to this desk,
As my screen flickers
my fingers tap the keyboard,
I've become
a piano player
of empty gestures.

I was on top
of their game yesterday,
but I'm only as
good as the
stock market says
I am today.

At night
me and
a few others
down their tumblers
numbing our chattering brains
with the opiate of cliched refrains
our elixir to pain.

You see when I am
84 floors up
my callused feet are still
cemented to
this goddamn floor
and I don't know
who I am anymore.

And all I can do
is watch those
morning birds soar.

Father Knows Best–Mother Does the Rest

~ based on the TV show

The bland tyranny
of the cardigan sweater.
His smile
creased in brutal condescension.
Mother corseted in apron strings.
Bud—
with a greaser's
black defiant lock
rushes to the freedom
of the front door.
Father calls
"Princess!"
and she arrives
dancing with the dog
with an anxious, scripted
girlish giggle.
And don't
you think
yhey would like to
kill him
just a little?

Curiosity Killed the Cat

A house cat escaped
ran a bit too far
died under
the maw of a
foreign car.

Why did he leave
his cushioned seat
for something so
abstract
on the street?

Just before he was hit
sniffing the pavement
for some arcane scent—
I wondered
what was his Holy Grail
that made him
slap his tail?

Mrs. Plant

An art teacher
at our elementary school
her face
a painting
that she worked on
for a long time.
An angry mask
of red lips—
and rouge.
Disappointment
sinking her cheeks,
she passed the
mimeographed sheets.

At night
I imagined
she sat
with an arthritic cat
and a shot glass
screaming at
the reproductions on
her walls.

Did she recall
when she
was clad in black
and, oh so
tragic and
enigmatic
taking feverish notes
by the paintings

on the Modern's walls,
walking back to
her cold water flat
sketches,
a love note
stuffed in a pocket
of her winter coat…?

The Suburbs, 1962

Mom
a gurgling scream
from the backyard.
Something had invaded
the Lilly of the Valley
penetrated the well-trimmed hedges,
had tread on
the impossibly-green
carpeted lawn.

Undoubtedly
a monster
something of that ilk
that lurked under my bed
a nocturnal nightmare
escaping to daylight
something one-eyed
requisite tentacles
in a fury of suction
and destruction.

I watched
the diminutive Black man
tumble through
a tangle of lawn chairs
falling at the pit of the barbecue.

My father and his friend
took their cue
whisking him away
white knights saving the day
whisking a spec of dirt
from the dreamy illusion
of our summer day.

Morning Birdsong

I hate it.
The cloying
cheap chirp
that you are enjoying.
The cheerful melody
amidst the nuclear plumes
yet the second wave
of monstrous waves.
There you are
out on a limb
you tweeting twits
you avian nitwits.
You ruffle
my feathers
dropping your
turds at dawn
on my manicured suburban lawn,
singing insanely—
oh, the pain, the pain.

At dawn
both my cat and I
stare at the sky
with ravenous eyes
helpless
as you belt out
your morning cries.

I Tried to Frame a River

I had an attractive frame
but it came apart at the seams.
Everything seemed flimsy.
It refused
to be hung out
To dry…
on some museum wall.
And fish jumped
on musical scales
doing a jitterbug
on the newly-polished floor.
I ripped,
and stripped
the canvas
from its mount
and washed it down the sink.
It seemed
to fit so well
not even a ripple
it was one with the current—
a stream?
Yes, that's it…
of enlightened consciousness.
A fluid wave of abstract brilliance.
No, they said
"It is a river,"
so reluctantly
I just let it flow…

Harvard Square Theater: The Last Picture Show

~ in response to this historic theater's closing in Cambridge, MA

To spend the dog days
in the darkened theater
my Last Tango in Paris
respite from the heat.

The midnight mass
of the faithful
the rituals
the memorized chants
to the *Rocky Horror Picture Show*.

I will grab a beer
from the ghost of the Wursthaus
then get a seat in the back
the flickering of the dark cinema
a two-hour balm
before I hit the hot street
then it's gone…

PORTRAIT OF AN ARTIST AS A YOUNG POSEUR
BOSTON 1974 – 1983

Father's, the North End

Oh that distinct flushed-out smell of Father's Five—tattooed, Hell's Angels, ready to bounce you at the door—the Citgo sign flashing in the canyon of Kenmore Square…a signpost…direction…an elixir to your fog—vinyls at Looney Tunes—the old ladies of Coolidge Corner in Brookline who brought you their dead husbands' shirts when you manned the counter—*This should fit you*, they crooned. And you would be a walking monument to the dead. Cutting through the alleys in the Back Bay—a buffet in the trash bins for the down and out—they delicately picked at the remains of the day, sewage and rot behind tony shops—it was always Doomsday on the Common—street preachers at a clearance sale—street singers—songs for change—begging for it. The old Italian guy who yelled at you at the Haymarket: *Hey Kid, ripe tomatahs, get one for yer tomatah.* Laughing, the stub of a cigar shaking outside his mouth. The Mass. Ave. Bridge…it gave your life a horizon—open space from the small furnished room. My city on the hill—Buzzy's Roast Beef—a knish-delish—hotdog—oh, red phallus of beef, melts in my teeth. Karen, the Jewish girl I met at the matzo ball, we danced, and coupled in her small, flat in the North End. You learned how to love and leave—Caruso music and the couple that had operatic fights in sync…Her last words before she threw you out: *I can't stand all this eating!* Smell of bread baking all night on Salem Street—corpulent men outside the social club—called you *twinkle toes*—as you jogged by on chicken legs. Your friend—a clerk—dating a dwarf—an adjunct at Boston College—American Studies—a small love affair…

Park Drive

Lived on Park Drive. Sounds fancy—but overlooked the subway tracks and the vast Sears warehouse—the roar of the subway, the gray, looming Sears trucks in the distance—the trickle of the Muddy River. My window open—forgot I was nude—catcalls from the subway platform at my flabby body—bloated from the 11 to 7AM shift at McLean—sitting watching the 4-point restraints on patients—-rise and fall—with sedated breath. I saw so many of those chests: inflated, defeated, and deflated. The croissants from the Savoy Bakery in Audubon Circle were flaky concessions, the dark beers and the dark, cavernous bar at Browns, my balm. And the elevated tracks on Harrison Avenue—elevated me—I was a transcendent blur crosstown. The Dudley Bus idling near the vacant lot, rats as big as cats foraging near a fence. Sometimes I met her at the Nickelodeon…was it *Kiss of the Spiderwoman*? Held her hand, traced it the way I would trace her body later in the studio—a rail-thin graphic artist from Providence—she wrote me beautiful letters that made me swoon in my room.

271 Newbury Street

Early in the morning—I heard the retired Irish civil servant…a pensioner with a stained undershirt and plaid boxers—coughing up phlegm—heard through the thin walls: *How are you, me boy?* he crooned at me in the morning—both of us jockeying for the head down the hall. Then the fire alarm—a gas main break—out in the street—explosions traversed Newbury Street. I ran down the stairs in my blue corduroy sports jacket—a slightly irregular affair—from the depths of Filene's Basement…padded shoulders to bolster my narrow ones and a frail ego—a waxed mustache—the guys in the real estate office on the first floor used to crack: *Well, Hello Dali!* I made my way down the winding staircase (the spinster on the second floor opened the door a crack—she knew she would be flushed out)—me—with a red scarf around my skinny neck—like a poor man's ascot—Kirby Perkins, the newsman on the scene—I heard him say from the side of his mouth to the cameraman: *Look at this fuckin' character.* So oblivious to my absurdity—a beret on my already thinning hair—a rakish angle—I could be a posturing mannequin in one of the shop windows—central casting-clichéd young Beatnik.

Copley Square, Ken's Deli

Copley Square—Midnight—slipped into Ken's Deli. A Jackie Gleasonish fat man—the manager—stationed by the rotisserie chickens—a chorus line of spread legs, melting flesh, wings posturing on their plump hips—wondering which one would I choose. A dishwasher emerged, effeminate man, dirty apron, a cigarette in a holder, long expressive hands, wearing an eye patch. Drag Queens in the men's room. At the counter on the first floor—a waitress—not long on patience piped: *What's it going to be, hon.* Actors off from a gig at the Colonial, gesturing to each other dramatically at the booths—a few years before—I was a dishwasher here. I was chosen from a lineup of world-weary men: *You, you and you*, at 5PM—peering at all this through stacks of dishes—all this would be mine one day—a late night character—laughing over corn beef and chopped liver on dark rye—with poets and writers, after a day of writing—joking like Dorothy Parker, my round table…my Algonquin Hotel. The men I worked with I knew would reappear again—even then taking mental notes—trying to construct a narrative of the chaos of my life.

McLean Hospital

First night on the psychiatric ward—he called me his finest creation. I was responsible for the thunder and rain outside—the snapshots of light that popped at the windows—checks on the quiet rooms—museum windows of mental illness—peep shows—all those colorful pink papers—the legal confetti that led them here. A woman took a drag on her cigarette—hollow and sunken chest filled—a woman of substance, until she exhaled. I remember she once grabbed a beautiful young male attendant—squeezing his body close to her—as if she was trying to capture something—his youth—the shock of blonde hair—his strong, undefeated body was now in her reach. An old Boston Brahmin, haughty and insane, asked me if there were cockroaches on the unit…I said no. *Good, you must treat them elsewhere*, she replied. She insisted I was the young researcher from the Panamanian League on Newbury Street—and the young woman, on the 11-7 shift ran from her room in the nude—we danced with this frenzied, beautiful sprite at 3AM—and she performed her swan song—now supine, sedated—restraints. And I talked with a young man—he said he had a correspondence with Allen Ginsberg—*I have seen the best minds of my generation destroyed by madness…*

Dr. Solomon Carter Fuller

I taught Black History in the South End/ Solomon Carter Fuller Mental Health Center. A Jewish boy from Long Island—they called me *homey*—I thought, *homely*. They said my sorry, sagging ass looked like it had a ton of bricks resting on it—I never thought about this—I made clandestine trips to the men's room, with a hand mirror to check on my ass—they were right. We took them to the pool on the lower floor—one boy swam with a finger in his ear—a phone conversation with the voices in his head—they were pleasant—the boy had a wild, resplendent smile. Walking down Harrison Ave., past Chico's Bodega, bags of pork rinds in the window, lottery ticket addicts milling around, the usual drunk sprawled out under the awning, down from Boone's Farm or Muscatel, walking down past the Shanty Lounge—had dinner at Asmara with my friend Tesfay—large Ethiopian flat breads, with exotic droppings of meat and vegetables. He spoke of revolution—handsome professorial beard—soft spoken, seemed to ponder each word I said—a minister now—back in Africa.

Rexall Drugs, Busing Crisis

Working at Rexall Drugs on Boylston Street during the Busing Crisis—blushing when they asked for condoms across the counter—the mad man in the blue blazer—coat of arms—bulging eyes—shock of dyed blonde hair, rushing in and out of the store—looking perpetually shocked—as if he'd stuck his hand in a socket. A long distance flirtation with a cute 18 year old girl at the soda fountain—the smile, and the retreat, the seduction and abandonment, thought I was in a Thornton Wilder play. I heard the owner say: *It is the rich, Jewish liberals from the suburbs that are causing the crisis*. And everything my Bronx, *shtetl*, pale of settlement (Oh how I loved her *kishkas*) grandma said about the *goys* was true. *Well, the Catholic Church has a lot of money too*, I said. And fired the next day—they said I was rude to a customer…a lesson in life.

Neisner's, Kerouac, Ginsberg, Etc....

Neisner's…on a break as an assistant manager trainee for a Big L Discount Store—made my way to the Bromfield St. entrance—slopping up corn chowder with cornbread... then down to Barnes and Noble on Washington Street. Glanced at a book—interesting cover—an endless road, with a setting sun—some guy named Kerouac. Then that rush—the possibility that I could hit the same road—leave tracks—leave the tendrils of a straight-laced suburban roots—that voice in me that pleaded for freedom—caged by conformity. I was an addict, injecting myself with *Dharma Bums*, *Town and Country*—Allen Ginsberg's mother's pubic, gray, rabbinical beard. I sported a Burroughs's fedora—habituating the Café Algiers in Harvard Square—leaving Beat books on the counter of the grocery store I worked in, at Brookline Village—hoping to provoke a discussion with a customer. Wrote stream of consciousness flourishes in my journals—posturing, unapologetic—as if I was admitted to the cabal—still not venturing much past Kenmore Square.

Jack's Joke Shop

Jack's, near the Common—your first Dick Nixon mask—all jowls, pointed nose, crowned with hate and Watergate. And the subversive Whoopee cushion—slip it on a seat—and hear the old fart clamoring to get up. Oh—and the clock: *No sex Until Six*—and that carnal circle of sixes. And way before you were a Glaucoma suspect—you could laugh as your eyes pop from your sockets on Slinky springs. You were still a boy—laughing at toys—not that far from boyhood joys.

Milner Hotel, Chinatown

It must have been near the Milner Hotel, an old fleabag at the time. And I was found out by an old black gent who watched me while I passed. He knew what my sorry ass was up to—how I made a mountain out of a fuckin' molehill, and save my chicken shit walk—the head tilting attitude—for someone who hasn't seen it before, and has time to give a good God damn. And I remember Chinatown—those late night meals at the Ying-Ying—the staccato chatter of the patrons—the roast ducks in the windows dripped fat seductively, the Chow Fun, greasy dollops of duck, swimming in broth—thick with noodles. I stared at the flashing neon outside the window, on the rain-slicked street. Rod Serling introduced me: *Have if you will, one Doug Holder…*

LAST NIGHT AT THE WURSTHAUS

Looking at a Lone Woman in a Bar

They are always so impenetrable.
A dead stare at the wall.
Her drink
some half-empty prop.
And the cigarette…
still holding a torch
but for what?

No—
my gaze will not be met.
And she will walk out the door.
And the clues
she will leave
a certain dead end.
And the cigarette will smolder
and the smoke
will follow its trail…

Filene's Basement, Boston

And the doors could barely contain them.
The thoroughbred ladies ready to race
at the stroke of the clock's hand
for discount linen and lace.

And I was swept in
by an animated, cackling
feminine wave,
soon eyeing
the salesman
eyeing me
as I was transformed—
polished into a well-heeled
businessman
in a double-breasted suit,
and the clerk cracked by my side
"Hey, kid, ain't she a beaut?"

And I fingered the starched
collars of multi-colored
Arrow shirts
and I admired the crusty, ancient saleswoman
who still had the desire and energy to flirt.

And where else
could you drape your wounds
with a funky Fedora
or the balm of a soft,
slightly irregular Brooks Bros. shirt
it was a place to go when you were happy
or desperately hurt.

Death of a Homeless Man

Last thing I remember
I laid on the grates
of the Boston Public Library
I was lifted up by
the waft of its
warm mist
I looked down
to a figure in a dirty parka
long nails like a raccoon
the intricate, matted mosaic
of hair.

I saw a woman
touch me with the cold
metallic tip of her
fashionable shoes.

Oh! Cradle me!
Cradle me in your arms!
I am not a stick
or merely a bone.

I was a boy running through a meadow
my skin smelled like baby's milk
my eyes were not clouds
but brilliant suns
I laid on my back
and searched the skies
like now
before I
died.

Blondes

They always will
intimidate you.
Even in your sixth decade—
those judgmental Barbies
blonde, blue-eyed
roll their eyes
and do a clandestine text
and yet
you still try to
win them over—

Stooped
your beard
white with regret
but you don't forget
the pain
and their pert disdain
in some ancient high school hall,
the pecking order
you clad in polyester
and body odor.

Oh, but you
are older
you teach with
glasses perched
on the bridge of your nose

your class
and you
in both your
early morning pose.

But you can't
bullshit the blonde.
She knows.

I Am Willy Loman

I hear my wife say,
"Attention must be paid…"
as I carried my heavy bags
each bag weighing down
my round shoulders
to her face.

"They love me, they love me in Somerville,"
I said to myself,
the wind's hollow howl
the cat's wide-eyed shock
his questioning meow
as I went out
to a 5 .AM. cold.

I had my shoes shined the other day
and pressed the threads
on my threadbare jacket
ready to plaster a smile
on my tired face
to shoot the same old shit
another round of pitches
bombast and bluster
for a few
brittle bones.

Sometimes those voices reappear—
my father
grabbing his morning vodka
from the icebox
"I think I failed you,"
he said.
Captured in dementia
and the maudlin.

It is another night
with Canadian Club
humming
under my breath
to Chet Baker's
"Let's Get Lost."

My cat
pounces on imaginary prey
and so do I.
I sip
and my night
will slip
to another
inevitable day.

My Mother Prepares Me for Death

She wants me to stay in a hotel
she hides in her home
like an old house cat
before her costume
a pasted on
public face.

At night
the murmur of the dead
hover around her bed.

She can't understand
what ails her.
Is the pain
in for a permanent
stay?

And the doctors croon,
"Take one of these, dear
you will feel
better soon."

We face each other
in a dark corner
of a
plastic suburban cafe.

We know what lies in
our receding gums
the tip of our coffee-
stained lips,
the fantasy of our
flesh.

In silence
we have said it all—
more or
less.

And
at night
the murmurs
of the dead
hover
around
her bed.

"Oh Don't," She Said, "It's Cold."

~ for Rita Holder

"I'm depressed
I'm old."

I held her hand
"Oh don't," she said.
"It's cold."

She said,
"Maybe I pushed too much
maybe I gave in much too soon,
perhaps it was something
I needed to be told."

I held her hand,
"Oh don't," she said.
"It's cold."

I said,
"But we love you
what was once bought
has now been long sold."

I held her hand,
"Oh don't," she said.
"It's cold."

She said:
"What should I have seen?
What was I meant to be?
What would have pleasured me?"

I held her hand:

"Too bad," she said.
"It's warm now
but oh so old."

Her hand
gently
broke from me
and like spotted moths
fluttered free.

The Lottery Ticket

In the Harvard Square Starbucks
he pops a prescription.
The coffee has long
gone cold.
A swirl of sour milk
pocks its surface.
His tickets
have been scraped
of any value.
And the *Herald*
crossword
is still
a puzzle.
every hour or so
he asks me to watch his seat
and he comes up
with another ticket,
and looks out the window
at a boutique square
his wasteland now.
He has got the itch
he scratches again
only to reveal
a dead-on-arrival number.
Another trip to the urinal
but hope springs eternal
and as he has done for years
he scratches
he scratches
at the
surface.

A Mother Leads Her Child to the Men's Room

And he takes her hand.
And walks into that room,
with all his reluctance,
and all its strange allure.
And it will be a woman who he will trust.
Who will teach
him the right way,
as he drops his pants
and releases a fine
and diffuse spray.

Lung Cancer, Stage 4

~ for Jim Resnick

We sat together
at Panera Bread.
He smiled
the spaces
between his brown teeth
corrupted his mouth,
the long chain
of smoking
tainted his skin
to cigarette ash,
his eyes
seemed
like they were
ready to pop from their sockets
to flee
the ruin of his body
before it collapsed.

I asked him:
"If you could do it again…?"
He said:
"I wish my parents
sent me to a private school."

And I thought of that child
blushing from the sweet taunts
from playmates
the calls of an elusive girl
from a distant corner,
a playground
on a sultry
summer afternoon.

All before
the lungs
took in
that lethal breath
that smoky, numbing sting,
to quell
the snake
that swirled
and ate him
from within.

A Dog Digging up his Master's Grave

One might think
it is just a dog
digging up a long-lost bone.
But
he is at the base of the tombstone.
Barking at the dates
of birth and death.
The paws are now blurs
this dog makes
the earth move
his nose drips
as if to water
something
that will
never
come
to life.

He wags his
dead end tail.
Trying to
Sniff out a scent
his cheap. cloying
aftershave
the cocktail hour whiskey
he liked it neat.

The dog in frustration
gnashed his
canine teeth
and falls asleep
right above
his master's
splayed
and decomposing
feet.

A Vacant Stare at the Sky

On the phone
my sister-in-law
her voice brittle and cracked
"Oh my God, a bomb at the marathon!"

At the radio
the Towers collapsed for me again
now—
the damning knapsack
…the white smoke
lower extremities
shrapnel
the reporters constant replay
and I am fixated
worried about my own sorry ass
and then something clutched my throat
as my friends' and family's faces
a cinema of wide-eyed fear
flashed before me
wondering
if they were
at the finishing line…
was it their time?
and when was
mine?

In the aftermath
that woman's vacant stare
at the sky
as if the heavens could answer

"Why?"

Living in Your Pajamas

And still
You adorn
the beat-up
slippers
the fuzzy formless
pants—
with their animals,
histrionic smiles
faded to jaded smirks.

Everything remains loose
you don't let things cling
Collared shirts try to define you
ties are snakes
around your thin neck.

Gerber stains
mix with Canadian Club
on your threadbare top

and it's too late to untie
you are in a knot.

The Big Bang

It's not the bang
so much
as the anticipation
the sensitive hairs
in each of your
expectant drums
your body
retreating into
its seminal
fetal curl
the hands'
feral clawing
and it all
boils
down to
some histrionic
exploding sun,
and then
quite simply
You're done.

NEW

Hitting the Right Note

a pregnant plunge
before the fat lady's
swan song
before the scatter and spray
of scat
before the moaning, sex of
the sax
before the be-bop
bleat of the horn,
the bloodshot eyes
leap in their sockets.

It makes their shot glasses wave
and tremble
clears their sinuses
their red- hot pepper
it's the stake that pierces
the pimento-eyed olive
the sucker punch
when you turned
away.

Obit

But he was 68 years old.
Only a few years older…
a twinge in his pancreas
dead in three months.

Or he was found on the toilet seat.
Cheap plaid boxers
under an expensive linen suit.

They found him propped in his favorite chair
in front of the TV
Archie Bunker said, "Ah, Jeez,"
and he was gone.

They were known for their kindness
but what a world we would have had.
These men and women
proud of their service
survived by many
as if it was an accomplishment
a son in Cleveland
a daughter in Dallas.

They were just a few years older
the black and white
post office face
that stares
at me
as a matter
of fact.

Meeting Allen Ginsberg (Buffalo, NY, 1975)

A middle-aged Jewish uncle
his bald dome
framed by graying locks
a tangled tapestry
draping below his ears.
The rhythmic slap of his hands
on the drum
his head raised to the ceiling
addressing some light
that only spoke his name.
"If you want to live, live.
If you want to die, die.
If you want to make love, make love."
The college radio manager
told me that he was a prophet
that I should interview him,
a boy with impossibly rosy cheeks
a faint mustache
the like that I have seen
on my maiden aunts.
I walked up to him
my shambling gate
the gone-to-seed
crowd around him
snickered at this
not yet defiled cherub
as I shook his hand
a hand I
never really
let go
of.

Where is my Pocketbook?

~ for Rita Holder

"I lived enough—
I've done it all."

She clutches her pocketbook
a weathered bag
to her weathered face.

Now it is resting
on her deflated breasts.

"This is unfair, I want to die!"

The light dims
an evening surrenders
she screams shrilly
at the institutional walls

"Where is my pocketbook!"

I give it to her
she rifles through the
plastic promise of
credit cards
the crumpled receipts
the scraps of paper
with deceased phone numbers.
and the faded stamp
of errant lipstick.

Her fingers
move
like an arthritic snake
in search for
a flimsy thread
to hold on.

"Why must I suffer?
Let me go."

"Where is my pocketbook?"

"Where is my pocketbook?"

I don't know why

i don't know why
i have visions of elevated tracks
subways defiantly roaring
at the dark
damaged men pawning costume
jewelry for cheap redemption
legless men
on wheeled carts
"can you spare
a fin?"
after all he was a former
choir boy.
the patrician slap of the old
gray lady on the pavement
outside the newsstand
a sign on a city street
sig klein fat men's shop
men in black overcoats
clandestine girth
hidden behind their
draping body armor.
the sliding shot glass
over the polished wood
monk's straight no chaser
in the background
the summer street
a kid throws his radio
out of a bronx tenement window

the yankees went south in the tenth.
a man at ratner's whose life has been
reduced to yelling at a round shouldered
waiter,
"you call this a pickle!"
the neon's ironic wink
all this sound
and fury—
must signify
something.

We Hold Hands

At dusk
we hold hands.
We hold hands,
with facing
tarnished rings.

As if some
unexpected storm
could suddenly
separate us forever.

We listen to the muted horn
the hint of some heroin-tainted voice
we clink our cocktails
the house cat
another appendage between us.

And the light grows dimmer
as it always does.

Texting in Class

They are like gymnasts
tapping below their waists
a resplendent smile to their crotch.

Their heads bob
up and down
a restless buoy.

I call on them
they smile with cunning innocence
a slight-of-hand
they slip
it clandestinely
into a pant pocket

something is up their sleeve.

There is always
a tapping subtext
in class.
My commentary
lost in their coded
text.

It should be on the syllabus
this game of cat and mouse.
But their bodies
shake
they are not
on firm ground.

Pyscho

The naked vulnerability
a threatening rustling of curtains
through the torrents of rain.
I still expect
the thrust
of the archetypal dagger
the noise outside the deluge
muddled, but with implicit danger
I grip the soap
it slips nefariously
from my hands
I bend over
such blind trust

Truro Beach

It was a figure of a woman
in the 5 A.M. mist.
Her hair waving in the wind
like a melodic line.
I found scattered sea glass
in her wake
shards that reflected me
in fractured moments of time.

An old crab followed me
we were both in our shells
suspicious narrow slits of eyes
he was some life-long crony
it could have been Jim.

A Greek Chorus of gulls
squawked at me to go on.

I finally reached her
and the crab and I watched
as they disappeared
in the mist.

The Mall

~ for Sheree Pollack

Oh—painted ladies
Oh—cosmetic ladies
offer me a make-over
give me the stiff
mask of Botox creams
give me that elixir
that will fix her
a fragrant mist
that will make
her an enigma
in black
once again.
Smile at me
yet again
with the cakes
of makeup
cracking like
fault lines
on your face.
Mannequins
you are so stilted
frozen in the midst
of some action
that will not
bear fruit.
Give me the polo shirt
you wear
on your hardened torso

I want its neat perfection
no loose ends
nothing frayed.
Oh—food court
with your gaggle
of teenagers
doing the twist
with their fingers
on their cell phones
their fast, breathless chatter
their food
twisted, breaded
creatures
that emerge from the depth
of a deep fryer.
I try to transcend it all
on the escalator
but the mall bitch slaps me
with an onslaught of brands
the sale, the discount
and finally
the clearance.
The green-haired
the pink-haired
nostrils flaring
with nose rings
they try to go
against this grain

but they plaster
the plastic floors
of Newbury Comics.
And back at the food court
the old lady flashed a senile smile
at the sizzle of the neon
and the approaching
night.

Guitar Man

And when he riffed
his girth
was no obstacle.
He rose
like beckoned
from above.
His head craned
like a meaty swan
following the music
like some
driven
Egyptian hieroglyphic—
face twitching
as if it
was synchronized.
His eyes tightly
locked
on the singers.
And
all I could see
were his
agile, manic
fingers.

Jacob Wirth (Boston, MA., 1868 to 2019)

The sawdust
on the floor
has gone the way
of all dust.

But it is the hard slap
of the house dark
on the dark, mahogany bar
that sustains me.

Yes,
they have made
concessions
to a high
definition TV
but the ancient
beaten ivories
of the piano
still hold its torch songs
on Friday nights.

And
it seems
there is still a wholesome, yellow statement
of cornbread,
and a saucer of
baked beans.

The long dining room
has stretched over 100 years
and in the rear
there is a pay phone
in its battered booth
before you hit the head.

And that din of laughter—
(and I admit
I miss the cigar smoke)
and the bright red—
sheaves of corned beef
sprouting from dark bread.

What was once alive in this city
is still
not quite
dead.

The Debutante of 1938

~ based on Dianne Arbus' photographs

A cigarette
hangs languidly
from her clawed hand—
her head tilted
in patrician amusement
her tortured eyelashes
flare out—
pricks of disdain.

Ozzie and Harriet
appear on the lawn
joined at the hip
blending into blandness
their smiles
hollow posturing for the
lens—

And there is the girl
eleven years old
so stiff
trapped in a crocheted
cocktail dress
a child
forced in a cage
of carnal contours.

The shutter
has long since clicked
and closed
the many doors.

Marijuana

When I could stare at a tree
and feel myself
covered with bark.
My twig arms
branches extended to the wind
my hands full of
spores.

And in that cornfield
the moon
an impossibly
bright orb
seemed to be
blessing me
at night
oh…
celestial light.

And each stalk of corn
waved
in waves
across the
long expanse
of the field.

I tried to
feel that way again
but nature…my nature
doesn't yield.

In My Mind I Swam to Spectacle Island

On the Boston Harbor Island ferry
our guide
told us about Deer Island
aptly named
a temporary haven
for deer
as they swam to escape
the trap jaws of wolves.

Now
a sewage dump
a treatment plant
a mole
festering in the water.

The ancient, escapist deer
of course
would eventually succumb
to a well-appointed
hunter's trap or
some deep wound
that ran as wildly
as they did.

In my mind
I swam to
Spectacle Island
the ferry
a prop
a figment in the ether
I was hoofing
it like a deer
through the harbor's choppy waters.

Reacquainted with silence
on a park bench
surrounded by
preening dandelions
looking
out at the eruption
of Boston's skyline
and all these predators
just waiting for me.

Canned

In a tin
the metallic flap
peeled away
like a skin
what a predicament
they are in.

All eyes
neat rows
well-oiled
packed in, like, well,
what they are.

I wonder
what school of
thought they
were in,
before their
terminal canning,
before this twist of fate—

what were they planning?

Master Lock

Oh! The revolutions we have been through.
The many different spins we have taken.
A turn to the right,
after our earlier flirtation with the left.
All these years—
just trying to
find something
that clicks.

The Hudson

A misty
broad sheet
of placid water
that enveloped
the fine, powdery
spray of
fallible flesh and
brittle bone—
all that
was left of
the man.

The river slowly
dragged him downstream
past the
worn, world-weary
Bronx tenements
of his youth—
then passing
the teeming city
he loved, left, but always returned to—
the very city
he cut his baby teeth in.

Finally
he was flushed out
to the
wide mouth
of the open sea
his essence—
where
he always
wanted
to be.

They told me…

that they will take my dust
the ash of my bone
the undifferentiated
gray—
wisp of flakes
and compress them
into diamonds.
I will ride
on someone's index finger
or perhaps
pierced into
my nephew's nose…
I will be all what I wasn't
hard, crystalline
angles
cold and brilliant
with the icy
charm of a sociopath—
something to look
forward to
when I am old

I am told…

A Tongue Sandwich

~ for Rita Holder

As a young Bronx girl
she bit the tongue
like she bit her own,
under the despotic
pale of settlement
repressed, Jewish, homosexual
father's nightly frenzy.

The beef tongue
pink
with the light white
flourish of taste buds
that she swallowed with a burst
of seltzer—
her sentencing every afternoon.

And the fare
never changed
it was pre-arranged
the tongue never flapped
on a piece of banal rye.

It was once
thick
with a cow's
mooing passion
now cut razor thin
and she ate it silently
in the Deli's
din.

Dreaming on the Senior Line at Market Basket

I walk with Ginsberg and Whitman
and we will talk.

I'll dream of tomatoes
rich red draping from a vine
my naked hands
feeling the
blush
of their,
rippling skin
I will bathe in
the wet jungle of grapes
bubbles of fruit
dancing on the contours
of my balding scalp.

Yes
I will join the bunch…

of bananas
that hang like a fruit bat
yellow and bruised
just to get in
under their peeling
skin.

I will tell them about the predicament we are in.

Vinyl, cloth and plastic
wrap the world
but I dream of mangoes
or a sad-eyed haddock
joyously twirled.

A Cap

Sometimes
I need it to
contain myself.
With a diverting
brand name
to hide the secret
perhaps
the shame.

A cap—
a snug
fit
for my
skull.

My scalp presses
against the seams,
Oh…
so many
schemes.

Bozo tufts
of gray hair
explode above
my ears,
a vein
on the side
of my head
pulsates with blood—

an angry artery
ravenous
glutted with
wanderlust
hungry
for escape.

There is something
beneath this cap
percolating
a pregnant bubble
beneath the skin,
something crying
for an out—
and then
an in.

If We Froze with a Fork in our Hand

Before we took the bait
and just before the bite
before we enveloped it with
our hungry breath
before the mindless flap
of our coated tongues
before we smashed it
with a new set
of porcelain teeth,
and the day to day
grind of our cracking jaws.

How about,
if we just
took a second
to simply

pause?

Made in the USA
Middletown, DE
19 June 2020